SYSTEMS

USING FIRST PRINCIPLES THINKING TO ADVANCE YOUR CAREER OR BUSINESSES

IDEAS FOR SMART PROFESSIONALS

COACH TEDDY EDOUARD

COACHING FOR BETTER LEARNING

This book is designed to offer guidance on career and professional development, but its teaching should not be taken as legal advice and services. If you need legal help, consult a licensed legal professional.

While Coaching for Better Learning LLC has made every effort to provide accurate information at the time of publication, neither the publisher nor the author assumes any responsibility for errors and changes that happen after the release of this book. The author and the publisher have no control over and do not assume any responsibility and liability for third-party websites and their content.

Copyright © 2022 by Coaching for Better Learning, LLC
Copyright © 2022 Teddy Edouard

All rights reserved.
Print ISBN: **979-8-362-29965-1**

CONTENTS

INTRODUCTION: Who should read this book? 1

CHAPTER I First Principles Thinking: Its Origin and Its Key Principles 6

CHAPTER II Concrete Examples of First Principles Thinking in the Business World 12

CHAPTER III Thought Leaders in First Principles Thinking 19

CHAPTER IV Why Embracing First Principles Thinking Is Vital for Entrepreneurs and Businesspeople 26

CHAPTER V Why Embracing First Principles Thinking Is Important for Professionals and Employees 34

CHAPTER VI Strategies for Developing First Principles Thinking Skills and Abilities 41

CHAPTER VII How to Use First Principles Thinking in Your Personal Life to Stand Out 50

CHAPTER VIII How to Stand Out Using First Principles Thinking in Your Professional and Business Life 58

CHAPTER IX Research, Tools and Other Resources on First Principles Thinking 66

CONCLUSION 77
REFERENCES 79
INDEX 80
ABOUT COACHING FOR BETTER LEARNING LLC 82

INTRODUCTION

Who should read this book?

This book aims to introduce professionals and entrepreneurs who want to be innovative and stand out from the crowd to *First Principles Thinking*. It offers them a set of guidelines or a system that they can apply to examine and tackle work and business problems or challenges.

At **Coaching for Better Learning (CBL),** we believe a good system is the key to stress-free improvement, growth and success. We also coach our clients on leveraging *First Principles Thinking* to create innovative solutions and rise above the competition in the marketplace.

We designed and developed this book for folks who do not want to waste their time using so-called "best practices," conventional thinking and popular beliefs to make decisions.

The book is limited to practical applications of First Principles Thinking (FPT) in the workplace and businesses. Therefore, it is not intended for readers who want to philosophize about and debate First Principles Thinking.

Simply put, this concise book is a practical tool for professionals, entrepreneurs and students who want to understand, practice and leverage their thinking to get ahead in life by finding creative solutions to daily challenges. It is about using innovative thinking to rise above the competition. It also encourages readers to think for themselves instead of letting the crowd or the media think for them.

CBL produced this book for people who have a strong desire to think and do better in the marketplace. The book is for those who need a step-by-step system to think for themselves so they can take the wheel, shape their career and choose their life work, instead of following popular trends.

In brief, this book may be for you if you

- ➢ **are tired of using conventional thinking** that supports the status quo.
- ➢ **want to think innovatively** instead of following best practices.
- ➢ **desire to lead**, instead of hiding behind "this is how we have always done things."

- ➢ **want to think on your feet** and sharpen your thought process.
- ➢ are **comfortable with being different** and misunderstood.
- ➢ **don't want to be a victim** of the crowd's biases and "wisdom."
- ➢ want to **sound informed**, cultured and enlightened.
- ➢ want to **stop living on assumptions** and superficial information.
- ➢ develop **sharp reasoning and critical thinking skills.**
- ➢ want to be **paid for innovative thinking** instead of getting a paycheck to maintain the status quo.

If the above list matches some of your interests and needs, keep reading! Let's go over what's included in this book.

Our Promise

This book on First Principles Thinking (FPT) is designed and written so that you can read it in one or two sittings. You can also focus only on the chapters that you believe will meet your immediate needs or help you establish your FPT system. In other words, the book is concise and straight to the point.

More importantly, the book teaches foundational knowledge about FPT and offers concrete examples and guidelines to help professionals and entrepreneurs work on building a *First Principles Thinking mindset* and system.

For example, this book contains a practical framework to help you start today. You should find enough information and resources to decide right away whether you will embrace First Principles Thinking as a way of viewing work and the world around you.

Additionally, CBL provides additional resources in the book for readers who desire to dig deeper and learn more about FPT to design their thinking system and game plan.

The book is organized into nine chapters.

Chapter 1	defines First Principles Thinking (FPT): its origin and key principles.
Chapter 2	presents concrete examples of FPT in the business world.
Chapter 3	presents thought leaders in FPT.
Chapter 4	discusses why embracing FPT is vital for entrepreneurs and businesspeople.
Chapter 5	discusses why embracing FPT is important for professionals and employees.
Chapter 6	shares strategies for developing FPT skills and abilities.
Chapter 7	discusses how to use FPT in your personal life to stand out. impacts one's personal, professional and business life.

Chapter 8 discusses how to use FPT to stand out in your professional and business life.

Chapter 9 shares research, tools and other resources on FPT.

Without further ado, let's dive in!

First Principles Thinking: Its Origin and Its Key Principles

"Boil things down to fundamental truths... and then reason up from there."

— *ELON MUSK*

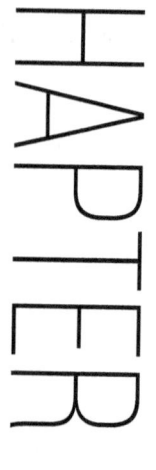

First Principles Thinking (FPT) is a philosophy used in science and mathematics. It focuses on the bare bones of why things occur and what is happening (the fundamental assumptions of an object). FPT involves starting from the basic layer or fundamentals rather than assumed facts or generally accepted knowledge.

FPT is sometimes known as the "bottom-up" approach. It is an inductive reasoning process that derives general principles from specific observations instead of top-down or deductive reasoning.

Deductive reasoning starts with a general principle and then seeks to apply it to a specific situation. In contrast, inductive reasoning starts with a set of observations or data and then attempts to find a principle that explains those observations. In other words, FPT is a way of looking at what's actually happening instead of trying to fit events into a preconceived system. In this chapter, we'll look at some of the key principles of FPT.

What Is the Origin of First Principles Thinking?

Understanding FPT requires us to travel back to its origins in ancient Greece.

FPT was initially developed by Aristotle as "first philosophy." First philosophy is used in science and mathematics. In physics, first principles refer specifically to foundational concepts in quantum mechanics.

Elon Musk, CEO of Tesla, has widely promoted the modern concept of FPT. He refers to this type of thinking as "reasoning from first principles" or "starting with the first principles." Today, FPT can be used in multiple applications in our daily lives, including in our business and personal lives.

Instead of making unfounded assumptions or accepting information blindly and at face value, you question them and challenge them if necessary. The aim is to continue building knowledge with an open mind to the possibility of being wrong and then adapting without taking anything for granted.

A Principles Thinking Framework

It is logical not to accept something as true until you verify its validity. This way of thinking helps you challenge notions and view things from a different lens and in a new light; it opens your mind to diverse possibilities that may arise from a paradigm change.

There are several fundamental principles in first principles thinking. Below is a framework or a set of guidelines that are used in FPT:

1. Find the problem.
2. Clarify the problem.
3. Break down the problem into its parts or layers.
4. Solve the problem.
5. Question the process.

When problem-solving, it's crucial that you start from a First Principles perspective. By using the "bottom-up" approach to solving problems, we can develop a complete answer that is often referred to as a *product architect approach*. This type of thinking involves first understanding foundations or basic layers before building something new.

For the First Principles Thinking process to be used correctly, all its parts must be correct. Each logical step of the process allows us to arrive at a solution or outcome with confidence—resulting in better solutions and outcomes overall.

SYSTEMS: USING FIRST PRINCIPLES THINKING

1. Find the problem.

Finding the problem is the first step for First Principles Thinking. To solve any problem, you must first understand the actual question that you are trying to answer. The problem itself usually looks more straightforward than it really is, and it can be hard to solve because of this fact.

For example, to find a cure for a disease, you need to understand all the contributing factors, including both biological and psychological aspects. If you don't know what has caused it in the first place or where the source lies, how can you ever hope to create a possible cure?

2. Clarify the problem.

After finding out exactly what the problem is, you will need to clarify why this issue exists. By understanding the problem, you can better understand the *root cause* of the issue. That way, you can approach a solution from a place where you can focus on building up strategies that will help you in this process and not blame or punish anyone because that won't get you anywhere.

The idea is to keep an open mind through all the steps involved with First Principles Thinking so you can strengthen your ideas and concepts by constantly challenging them.

3. Break down the problem.

To solve any type of problem, you must break it down into smaller pieces or layers. By breaking down a large, complex task, you'll be able to understand the process better and progress toward arriving at a final solution. This step is indispensable in FPT.

4. Solve the problem.

By using First Principles Thinking and following the previous steps in order, you'll be able to solve the problem and arrive at your desired outcome. The aim is to increase your likelihood of success when approaching problems in this manner. If you follow these steps, you can work more reliably and with greater understanding. Remember, you want your *knowledge to be as complete as possible,* so when you arrive at a solution, it will hold up under scrutiny and be valid for everyone involved.

5. Question the process.

Questioning the process is a crucial part of First Principles Thinking. In the past, we have been taught that following a specific process will always yield us a certain outcome - but this isn't true in every situation. Defining processes will help you arrive at solutions for problems. Still, it's also important to remember that each situation is different and requires its unique approach and its own problem-solving process depending on the variables at play.

In brief, FPT is a useful tool to have in your arsenal of problem-solving skills and techniques. By following a logical process, you'll be able to arrive at conclusions based on your intelligence and understanding. The process allows you to make solid decisions that are well-reasoned and can withstand the test of time when exposed to other opinions

SYSTEMS: USING FIRST PRINCIPLES THINKING

and perspectives; it's the most effective way to help you make business decisions or decisions that impact your career.

Though it may take more effort in the short term, using First Principles Thinking can save you significant amounts of time in both your personal and professional life, allowing you to spend less time worrying about problems and more time working towards solutions!

Let's go over some examples in the following chapter.

Chapter 1: Concrete Examples of First Principles Thinking in the Business World

"Indeed, the single most powerful pattern I have noticed is that successful people find value in unexpected places, and they do this by thinking about business from first principles instead of formulas."

— PETER THIEL

By using First Principles Thinking (FPT) and focusing on logic instead of preconceived notions, you can gain an understanding beyond surface knowledge about what is happening around you.

Elon Musk, CEO of Tesla Motors and SpaceX, most notably put forth First Principles Thinking in the modern business world. By doing this, he helped people make decisions based on reasoning instead of superficial or pre-existing assumptions.

Using FPT in the world of business is a good way to remain prepared for complex situations and avoid mistakes. This chapter will explore multiple examples of FPT in the modern business world.

How Is First Principles Thinking Utilized in Business?

First Principles Thinking can be a very powerful tool in the business world because it uses logic and reasoning to analyze each problem or situation. It allows you to approach the problem from a logical standpoint by setting aside any preconceived notions, biases or assumptions that you might have previously made about the problem.

Many successful entrepreneurs, CEOs, and their employees use FPT. Using the fundamental principles allows you to avoid assuming anything about situations and problems, so you only focus on their core truths.

Elon Musk has spoken extensively about utilizing FPT in the modern business world. As a highly successful entrepreneur, he states that many entrepreneurs have failed because they have made assumptions that were not necessarily true. When using FPT, you are using your logic and reasoning instead of relying on false preconceived notions to understand what is happening.

Elon Musk regularly uses First Principles Thinking to make decisions for his companies. For example, he designed the electrical system for Tesla by determining what would be best for its usage, rather than following others who had designed similar systems before him. Musk's goal was to produce an electrical system far superior to others, following his goal of creating the "best" car.

This example shows how Elon Musk used First Principles Thinking to decide what was truly best for Tesla, rather than simply making assumptions about how the company should run. It meant that he had to research more, but the extra work was worth it.

First Principles Thinking in Business

Using First Principles Thinking helps entrepreneurs, business leaders and those around them avoid dangerous mistakes caused by false assumptions or biases. Using this practice allows for more profitable companies and happier employees who feel as though they are working toward a logical goal determined by sound reasoning.

By utilizing First Principles Thinking in the modern business world, you acquire a natural advantage over those who rely only on surface knowledge, best practices and past experiences when making decisions. With this technique, you make sure you use your understanding and opinions to create new ideas, avoid costly mistakes and achieve career success.

Amazon's Use of First Principles Thinking

Jeff Bezos, the CEO of Amazon, also frequently uses First Principles Thinking when analyzing business decisions. Bezos has stated that using this technique allows him to be prepared for any situation or problem by not making assumptions about anything. Instead of relying on past experiences or surface knowledge of a business, he only analyzes the underlying fundamental truths of what is happening so he can make an informed decision.

Amazon is constantly utilizing FPT when making business decisions. For example, when developing their Kindle e-reader, they did not rely on mockups. Rather, they built actual prototypes to find out what customers wanted from the devices. After, they analyzed these prototypes based on the hard data they collected about customer needs and desires. Finally, they created the Kindle Fire. Using this process allowed Amazon to create a product that was able to stand out from the competition and become a bestseller.

Execution of the Model S Progressive Debut Strategy

Tesla Motors, an electronic car company, was facing problems with their flagship model, the Model S, which they were trying to break into the luxury car market for electric vehicles. Many issues plagued the early production runs of the Model S, including the following:

> ➢ Doors that wouldn't open and close
> ➢ Faulty rear seats
> ➢ Dysfunctional charging adapters

Elon Musk, CEO of Tesla Motors at the time, knew every one of these issues inside out because he had personally overseen every detail of the car's development.

While some people would be upset to learn their product has visible flaws after they spent so much money on it, Elon

Musk took it as an opportunity to use First Principles Thinking. He knew that despite the bad PR from these flaws, he could make the Model S better than all other cars on the market with this information.

Model S continued to be refined over time and now competes with some of the best luxury cars on the market. Today, it has many features not available in any other car, such as an all-glass panoramic roof and doors that open at the push of a button.

Utilization of First Principles Thinking by SpaceX

SpaceX also uses FPT when making cost-effective decisions for their business. SpaceX does not rely on traditional technologies to make rockets. Instead, they analyze the fundamental truths behind what makes a space rocket work and use those concepts to create more efficient designs.

One of Elon Musk's goals with SpaceX was to reduce the cost of launching a space rocket from tens of millions of dollars per launch to the range of $1 million per launch or less. To do this, he looked at what made up a space rocket and then analyzed each part to find out if it could be produced more efficiently. He would even take components apart in his free time to see how they worked before deciding if he could develop them further.

As a result, SpaceX developed reusable rockets, saving the company millions of dollars per launch. Their rockets also have more efficient engines, which carry heavier payloads at a lower cost than competitors, Boeing and Lockheed Martin. One of SpaceX's ultimate goals is to take astronauts to Mars, which would not be possible without their advancements in rocket technology. Their technique also creates many new jobs within the industry.

Targeting an Emerging Market with First Principles Thinking

Google is one of the biggest names in technology innovation today. Google often searches for new markets to enter by targeting emerging markets where they can provide value while staying aligned to their core competencies.

For example, Google created the Android operating system, which is now used on over 1 billion devices every year. They achieved this by recognizing an opportunity to provide software for mobile (smart) phones when most people were still connecting to the Internet through desktop computers. This decision was made after examining the existing market need and analyzing how the company could build upon current technologies using its core competencies.

Google's decision was successful as they were the first to target an emerging market where people were looking for an innovative solution. This choice changed them from being another run-of-the-mill search engine to become one of the most recognized companies globally.

How First Principles Thinking Eliminates Biases for More Profitable Businesses

While it may seem as though FPT is only useful for those who want to start new companies or work on cutting-edge technology, this technique can actually benefit anyone looking to make better decisions and succeed within an organization.

By utilizing First Principles Thinking in the modern business world, individuals have an advantage over those who only rely on superficial knowledge and experiences when making decisions. One of the benefits of First Principles Thinking is that it eliminates biases, which are often derived from past experiences, emotions and other factors. By using FPT, your thinking remains objective and grounded, thus making you more desirable to companies looking for someone who can make their businesses profitable.

The previous examples of companies applying FPT demonstrate the importance of using reasoning that goes beyond pre-existing assumptions and surface-level knowledge. To make progress in the modern business world, you can follow a philosophy utilizing FPT when approaching problems and making decisions.

FPT allows you to separate yourself from others who take safer approaches and follow existing thought processes and pre-established ideas. Using FPT in a business context allows you to focus more on logic instead of beliefs to avoid mistakes caused by surface-level assumptions and improve creativity when producing products.

Thought Leaders in First Principles Thinking

For we do not think that we know a thing until we are acquainted with its primary conditions or first principles, and have carried our analysis as far as its simplest elements."

— *ARISTOTLE*

First Principles Thinking (FPT) involves assessing the fundamental truth of a proposition and then reasoning from that proposition to gain new knowledge, derive conclusions or construct new arguments about that topic. In our modern world, some well-known thought leaders have used FPT in their work.

Some of the most influential thought leaders in First Principles Thinking are Elon Musk, Jeff Bezos, Peter Thiel and Richard Feynman. They've all spoken about how and why they use First Principles Thinking.

These thought leaders have used FPT to develop novel approaches to some of the world's most complex problems. This chapter will detail some of the best examples of how they have used First Principles Thinking in the modern world of business.

Elon Musk, Tesla and SpaceX Founder, on First Principles Thinking

Elon Musk is an American business magnate, investor, engineer and inventor. He is the founder, CEO and CTO of SpaceX; co-founder, CEO and product architect of Tesla Inc.; and co-founder and CEO of Neuralink.

Musk has said that one secret to his success using FPT is to be able to switch from idea to idea without getting stuck in any rigid patterns or frameworks. He says this practice allows him to move quickly within "a framework" instead of slowly.

Elon Musk has spoken openly about his use of First Principles Thinking in interviews and talks. According to Musk, First Principles is a practical way of looking at the world. You boil things down to the most fundamental truth and then use reason from there. This method allows individuals to identify the problem earlier than if they were reasoning by analogy.

For example, Elon Musk's work with Tesla Motors was based on applying first principles reasoning to cars by reducing them down to their most fundamental functional components (electric motors instead of internal combustion engines), identifying the best use cases for those components (long-distance driving), and using this logic to determine whether an electric car made sense (yes).

This way of thinking allowed him to make multiple accurate predictions. He understood how much it would cost to produce these vehicles (he estimated $30,000 for a Tesla Model 3 at the 2010 Detroit Auto Show), but he also predicted that the market would be opened to purchasing them. And as it turns out, he was right on both counts.

Jeff Bezos on First Principles Thinking

Jeff Bezos is an American technology entrepreneur, investor and philanthropist. He is the founder, chairman, (former) CEO and president of Amazon.com, which is today the largest retailer in the world measured by revenue and capitalization. Jeff Bezos also owns Blue Origin, which focuses on solutions for space travel; plans are in place for commercial suborbital human spaceflight.

Bezos believes that critical thinking skills are "a precious asset" when solving problems using FPT. This way of approaching issues allows individuals to pick out what's essential and disregard irrelevant data, allowing for more efficient problem-solving. It prevents decision paralysis and clarifies other possible solutions by forcing individuals into testing assumptions faster.

For example, Bezos required all new Amazon employees to perform a simple test where they would get an idea to improve the workplace, test it out and record the results. This test allowed all employees to start with a base assumption of how their process worked to identify where something went wrong. They could then create a quick system for problem-solving.

Other examples of his FPT include basing Amazon's warehouse design on customer needs rather than existing paradigms or taking advantage of machine learning by hiring experts in that specific area instead of building up an entire team with generalists.

Jeff Bezos's First Principles Thinking has been credited with the incredible success of Amazon.com and is a clear testament to its effectiveness when used correctly. According to him, "If you double the number of experiments you do per year, you'll double your inventiveness." This quote makes sense when looking at his experimentation process as it built Amazon.com into the Internet behemoth it has become.

Peter Thiel on First Principles Thinking

Peter Thiel is an American entrepreneur, philanthropist and venture capitalist. He is also co-founder of PayPal, Palantir Technologies and Founders Fund. His book, *Zero to One*, discusses how startups can use FPT to outperform existing companies.

Specifically, he argues that a significant advantage of startup companies is their ability to create something new instead of copying what already exists and competing with larger corporations with built-in advantages in certain fields.

Peter Thiel has been outspoken about his aversion toward modern education, which fails to encourage creative learning and critical thinking skills. He believes that all students should learn the basics of entrepreneurship and develop their success plans by thinking critically. In this way, students are more likely to discover what they enjoy because it will be something they've studied. They won't have to find "happiness" by following the footsteps of previous generations.

Peter Thiel refers to this mindset as First Principles Thinking, which he uses to approach everyday problems with an open mind. He advocates not limiting yourself with existing theories but instead forcing assumptions into action until you successfully prove your theory. It may take time to find the right theory, but this process speeds up innovation.

Richard Feynman on First Principles Thinking

Richard Feynman (1918-1988) was an American theoretical physicist known for his work in quantum mechanics, the theory of quantum electrodynamics, and particle physics. Throughout his life, he received numerous awards, including the Nobel Prize.

Feynman also became well-known for a teaching style that allowed him to break down difficult concepts into basic ideas by using everyday examples so students could easily understand.

He viewed FPT as a major component of creative thinking, which allowed him to connect difficult concepts so they made sense to students who may have otherwise misunderstood or believed false concepts.

Feynman provided two valuable tips for learning to think critically:

1. Give the problem a lot of thought before trying to solve it.
2. Make sure you are not deceiving yourself.

Using Feynman's advice, it makes sense that teaching students to think critically about their surroundings would help them develop creative thinking skills. This is because they will have a better foundation of knowledge to explore new ideas derived from First Principles Thinking. By following in his footsteps, these students might be able to understand the world on a deep level.

The Basics of First Principles Thinking in Business

FPT is the process of understanding a problem by first identifying the fundamental facts and elements relevant to it. The point of FPT is that instead of making decisions based on analogies, individuals should base their decision-making processes on underlying fundamentals.

The process starts by asking, "What are all possible ways this could be solved?" instead of reasoning by analogy that begins with, "How do we solve this like something else?" This way of thinking allows for better logical problem-solving and improved critical thinking skills, which can help reform flawed assumptions about problems.

This FPT method has been used successfully in many scientific fields, including physics and biology because it

SYSTEMS: USING FIRST PRINCIPLES THINKING

requires individuals to think critically about abstract ideas before applying them to real-world situations.

In the world of business, FPT can help create a better environment for corporations to grow because it encourages innovation. It also empowers members of a business to give their input on how the company should do things without feeling overwhelmed by hierarchy or convention, better leveraging the collective creativity of the company. This way of thinking is very common in Silicon Valley, where entrepreneurs are encouraged to develop their own solutions before seeking out investors.

While many thought leaders in different fields have used FPT to great success, Feynman is an excellent example of how the process can be incorporated into education. By developing a fundamental understanding of how things around you operate, students are better able to think critically about the possible ways that problems could be solved instead of following what worked for someone else. They can learn from mistakes made by those before them and give their ideas legitimacy because they have a complete understanding of the underlying concepts.

Why Embracing First Principles Thinking Is Vital for Entrepreneurs and Businesspeople

"The shortest and surest way of arriving at real knowledge is to unlearn the lessons we have been taught, to mount the first principles, and take nobody's word about them."

— HENRY BOLINGBROKE

FPT is a way of thinking that allows you to look at a situation from the ground up and then break it down into its most basic parts or principles. It starts by looking at the fundamentals rather than working with assumptions based on previous knowledge.

Embracing First Principles Thinking is important for entrepreneurs because it allows them to rise above the assumptions and preconceptions that dictate how others think, so they can start thinking objectively.

This way of thinking becomes especially useful when entrepreneurs are presented with new problems or difficult choices, such as deciding whether to expand into a neighboring city, which may require hiring more people or opening a line of retail stores, which would be expensive.

In this chapter, we'll explore the true importance of First Principles Thinking for business people and entrepreneurs.

When Is First Principles Thinking Useful for Entrepreneurs?

FPT is important for business people because it forms the basis for making decisions and solving problems in day-to-day work.

It can become useful when deciding between two options, solving key issues with your business, and making forward-thinking, effective decisions in how your business operates.

FPT also allows you to think about problems in a unique and novel way, which is necessary for entrepreneurs and business people who must innovate and push boundaries to create value in the modern economy.

One example is using this type of thinking when choosing a candidate to hire. If you restrict yourself to experienced employees, you may be missing out on new perspectives and opportunities that could allow you to create products and services with a competitive advantage.

However, it's not so simple as always hiring someone new to the field. Hiring an inexperienced candidate without the right traits would also inhibit your ability to innovate due to their lack of experience or understanding of what it means "to think outside the box." This reasoning shows how important it is for entrepreneurs and business managers to embrace FPT when making decisions, as it can lead to breakthroughs and innovation.

FPT is the process of understanding key parameters by which a problem you are trying to solve, or an opportunity you are trying to exploit, can be best understood. As Elon Musk puts it: "You boil things down to the most fundamental truths … and then reason up from there." The strength of this approach is that it doesn't get bogged down in extraneous details but instead focuses on what matters most.

It's an intuitive way of thinking that can lead to powerful advances because once you grasp the core idea behind something, you'll understand how all the pieces fit together. This means you can move forward with better foresight into where your product, vision or business plan is headed next and recognize what you need to do to take it there.

What are the Benefits of First Principles Thinking for Entrepreneurs?

FPT is essentially the best way to think about anything complex. You break down a problem or system into its core parts without getting distracted by irrelevant details. Then, you reassemble those pieces to understand them better. You can then solve the problem or better understand the opportunity you are trying to exploit.

SYSTEMS: USING FIRST PRINCIPLES THINKING

The benefits of First Principles Thinking for entrepreneurs include the following:

- A higher success rate in starting and growing businesses
- The ability to avoid pitfalls surrounding "paradigm paralysis" (sticking with the way things are currently done because it is comfortable, not ideal)
- The boosted ability to think of new products, services and business ideas that you can then build plans around
- Higher success rates in forecasting future trends and events
- The improved ability to take actions will improve your business without requiring outside confirmation from sources such as focus groups, polls, etc.

FPT is also useful for other areas of life, such as career advancement and planning. It is "first-order reasoning." Therefore, you come up with the idea that has never been invented before. Then, you break down the idea into its components to determine what makes it unique and special.

This allows you to build a system that works around your new idea. Using FPT, you can then ask yourself the following:

- How would I go about solving this problem?
- What does each part do?
- What assumptions am I making with my design?
- How can this be improved?

By stepping back from the problem and looking at it from all angles, those using FPT benefit from an ability to control the components of their design. They question everything, even if this means contradicting previously held assumptions about the world.

How Can Entrepreneurs Apply First Principles Thinking in Practice?

FPT is important for entrepreneurs and business people because it allows them to gain clarity on problems that have never been solved before, allowing them to break free from known patterns of thinking that prevent progress. It also adds depth and understanding that many who do not use FPT miss out on.

To use FPT in practice, entrepreneurs and business people can grow their businesses by improving their understanding of market conditions—from where current assumptions originate and how they affect behavior.

Those using FPT are invaluable in today's fast-paced and disruptive economy, where companies must constantly innovate and improve their products and services to stay relevant.

Real-World Examples of First Principles Thinking

Using FPT can be a powerful tool when used effectively in the business world. An excellent example comes from Tesla Motors' CEO, Elon Musk. He is known for applying FPT to his business challenges and, in doing so, has managed to launch multiple successful companies—Paypal, SpaceX, and Tesla Motors.

When launching Tesla Motors, one of Musk's biggest strategic obstacles was that electric cars were considered toys by many people at the time. The common belief was that they would never become mainstream alternatives to conventional cars. Because of this challenge, Musk continuously asked himself whether his assumptions about electric cars were true.

Musk eventually concluded that most of what people knew about electric cars was based on false assumptions rather than facts because they lacked information.

This process of questioning his assumptions led Musk to a major breakthrough: he realized that electric motors were far superior to those used in gasoline-powered vehicles. When combined with the fact that batteries were improving exponentially, he knew that there was no reason why electric cars could not become better than gas-powered ones.

The outcome of his series of questions and answers was Tesla Motors, which launched its first car—the Roadster—in 2008 and announced its plans to launch a second and more affordable model, called Model S, in 2009. Initial production was slow and early models had a variety of flaws. However, despite these setbacks, Tesla made a profit, and their stock price has been steadily increasing ever since.

Musk is not alone in his use of FPT; indeed, it can be seen as a common theme among many successful entrepreneurs today. Jeff Bezos, the founder of Amazon, is well known for his obsession with simple abstractions. For Bezos, it is easier to invent by looking at the fundamental truths behind a question—not by applying knowledge from the past. This simplified approach to finding solutions has also been applied to Amazon's latest project, AWS (Amazon Web Services). Instead of creating specific products for each service offered on their cloud platform, Bezos used FPT and instead decided to offer computing power via one product.

FPT can also be applied to more traditional businesses. The Four Seasons hotel chain, for example, is known as one of the most luxurious and innovative hotels, but it wasn't always that way. The company's founder, Isadore Sharp, had to think beyond traditional assumptions about service levels and amenities.

He challenged his staff to question their existing definition of "service" by asking themselves, "What does service mean?" This questioning led them to introduce customer access buttons in every room that allowed guests to order room service or request housekeeping with a simple push of a button—something unheard of at the time because most hotels only offered housekeeping services during working hours and charged guests for any additional services.

FPT has been used by numerous people for centuries, especially those asked to do the impossible or improbable. These people look at a situation through the lens of logic rather than going with their gut instinct, which is usually based on preset biases. This line of thinking is also often used when solving complex mathematical problems.

SYSTEMS: USING FIRST PRINCIPLES THINKING

A common trend in business today is for people to learn theories about how things work and what the "best practices" are in various situations; however, this can make us less open-minded to new ideas when we encounter them. It's inefficient because you may think your understanding of certain concepts is sufficient without truly understanding why they exist.

CHAPTER V

Why Embracing First Principles Thinking Is Important for Professionals and Employees

"You are stripping away each layer to get to the core of your problem. This is your call to adventure, figure what your fundamental problem is. From there plot your journey, select your quests, overcome your challenges, and make sure they lead to an end goal that you truly want to reach."

— ALBERT VAN DER MEER

Serious and well-informed professionals and employees should understand what First Principles Thinking (FPT) is and how it applies to their careers. FPT is a way of looking at the problem that allows professionals and employees to ignore currently accepted ideas and standard practices and focus on underlying truths.

Embracing FPT is important for professionals and employees at every level because it allows them to think more creatively and clearly, leading to better business outcomes and career advancement.

SYSTEMS: USING FIRST PRINCIPLES THINKING

The biggest challenge for professionals and employees is relinquishing their assumptions to see what's truly important, as opposed to what has been ingrained in them by convention or habit.

This chapter will go through a few examples of FPT that illustrate how it can apply to different professions. We'll then offer some suggestions on how professionals can adopt this mindset if they want to keep their careers moving forward.

What is First Principles Thinking, and Why Is It Important for Employees?

"First principles" refer to elementary or foundational elements of an idea, system or method on which everything else is based. They are an analysis tool used in fields like philosophy, physics, mathematics and economics that applies logic and reason to break down problems into more manageable parts.

People might be surprised by how many industries use the principle of FPT without even realizing it. For example, scientists will often use an approach known as "First Principles" reasoning when conducting experiments.

First-principles thinking involves focusing on first causes or "first principles" when examining a system or concept. This means the focus is not on things such as previously developed theories, hypotheses, models or preconceived notions about the systems involved.

By understanding these foundational elements of an idea or system, you can better analyze it despite prior assumptions, biases, conventional wisdom or anything else clouding objective judgment. This is because the first principles of a system are its most essential characteristics, and they cannot be reduced any further.

Employees and professionals should embrace FPT as it can help them develop a deeper understanding of their work and the theoretical foundations that shape it.

How Can Employees and Professionals Apply First Principles Thinking in the Workplace?

The implications of FPT for professionals are enormous because it helps them make sense of complex problems and develop solutions that work.

First Principles Thinking forces you to take a step back from the situation under examination and look at its underlying elements or principles. For employees and those in training, using FPT can help them become better problem solvers.

To apply First Principles Thinking in a workplace setting, follow these steps:

1. Find the problem.

Determining the problem is the first step in First Principles Thinking. Identify something bothering you, such as an issue with the company or a workplace situation. Asking, "Why?" helps you drill down to the basics of an issue and determine what is going on; asking, "How?" helps you determine how things can be improved or fixed. It also enables you to think of alternative ways to approach a problem without breaking established rules or procedures.

2. Clarify the problem.

Clarifying the problem is key to successful FPT. Define your question and determine if you can answer it with a simple "yes" or "no." For example, "Is this the best product we could be producing?" is not as clear as "What would make our product better than any other on the market?" It is important to be as specific as possible to avoid being overwhelmed with big-picture questions.

When you clarify the problem, you can also determine if you can answer your question by collecting data. If your answer to a yes-or-no question is not clear-cut, then it might not be appropriate for FPT at that time. You will need to collect data to gather sufficient information to come up with an answer and re-evaluate whether the process makes sense through FPT later.

3. Break down the problem.

To break down the problem means to take the initial issue or dilemma and break it down into smaller components. People make assumptions every day in all walks of life, including business. However, many people don't realize that they're doing so. You are making assumptions when you plan on taking a general direction but have not mapped out the details. It's important to ask yourself what your assumptions are before trying to solve any issues through FPT.

After writing out all your assumptions, evaluate them one-by-one until you either find an assumption where there is no agreement or consensus among other professionals or employees or an assumption where something could potentially go wrong.

4. Solve the problem.

Solve your problem by determining how it can be fixed or minimized without making assumptions. However, don't forget about your previous assumptions about this problem. Simply proceed with caution and recognize that your previous assumptions may have been incorrect if the problem hasn't gone away yet.

It's important to note that FPT is a refinement process, meaning you will need to go through this process multiple times before solving your problem. You cannot expect to end up with the perfect solution after only going through the process once or twice. Embrace iteration!

Consider Apple's invention of the iPod. Through FPT, Apple created a product that could store a thousand songs in your pocket, something that was considered impossible before the iPod was invented. The idea for this product came about through asking questions such as, "What are the functional components of a song?" or "How can we organize these components to fit in someone's pocket?" Apple asked these types of questions instead of trying to improve upon existing products.

Similarly, Google's search algorithms were born out of FPT. Larry Page and Sergey Brin originally wanted to create a system that would rank web pages based on their content without any consideration for the page's ranking in other search engines. This would have been an impossible task if they had not started with FPT because it questioned many assumptions about how to rank websites prevalent at the time.

5. Question the process.

What is the process you are following? Is it practical or efficient?

Asking these questions will help break down big problems into smaller ones. One should always try to simplify problems by breaking them down into their most fundamental parts. This allows you to figure out which rules need to be broken and what needs to be changed so that you can solve issues more effectively.

It's essential to question how things are done because commonly used methods often do not make sense logically but have become habits over time. FPT is essential because it's not just about getting more done in less time but also coming up with original ideas to arrive at solutions for difficult problems.

With this technique, Tesla was able to enter the car industry. They focused on what everyone else had ignored about electric cars—their limited range before needing a recharge. Being innovative means being willing to take risks, which comes from the freedom of having nothing left to lose. People who have accumulated a lot can become complacent, while those who are struggling will always be trying new ways of doing things.

FPT is not just for inventing new products or brainstorming, though. Elon Musk used FPT when he was trying to determine why rockets blow up so frequently. He came up with the idea of landing a rocket vertically by having it land on legs when no one else thought that would be possible because "no one had done it before." It took many iterations (remember that FPT is an iterative process!), but finally, SpaceX successfully landed a rocket vertically in December 2015. Since then, they have been able to reuse their rockets repeatedly, which has saved them millions of dollars. Innovation such as this was only possible by starting with FPT and eliminating all assumptions about what will make rockets successful or why they are built the way they are today.

When employees use FPT, they can break down problems and create better solutions, allowing companies to thrive in a competitive environment.

It doesn't matter the industry; FPT is useful for all professionals who want to attain success by breaking through assumptions about their work.

The most effective people start with the endpoint as a given, accept it as their starting point, and proceed logically, identifying new data along the way that requires changes to create better solutions.

Strategies for Developing First Principles Thinking Skills and Abilities

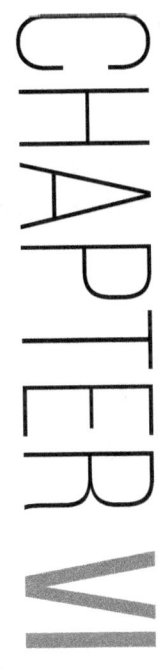

"When you reason from first principles, you do your best to ignore conventional wisdom and your own preconceptions, and you focus only on fundamental facts. You treat those core facts— the "first principles"—like puzzle pieces, and using only those pieces, you employ rationality to puzzle together a conclusion."

— *Tim Urban*

Often, FPT is preferable when approaching a task or solution. This thinking strategy frequently leads to a superior outcome and provides guidance on problem-solving and thinking about future opportunities.

First Principles Thinking is not something most people practice doing, but it can be developed and improved through practice, brainstorming sessions and hard work. Developing an FPT approach requires you to rid yourself of old thinking patterns from previous problems, solutions and best practices.

Being willing to let go of the past and seeing opportunities in new ways is often difficult for people to do. However, it can be done by anyone with a bit of determination.

How Can First Principles Thinking be Developed?

FPT is the process of taking something apart from its core elements to reassemble it into a different form. The goal is not just to change the details but to take apart the whole idea and rebuild it with new fundamentals. This mode of thought can be applied beyond problems that involve large concepts or systems and can be used in any situation where we might struggle because we're caught up in our preconceived notions.

To develop and practice FPT, you need to follow a clear framework in most situations. Your FPT should include action items and anything you judge necessary in your context. The following is an example of a framework.

FRAMEWORK

The Problem: Understand the problem and its impact within its context, time and culture.

Status Quo: Identify the status quo and traditional thinking used to attempt to solve the problem.

Fundamentals: Collect data and information that facilitates breaking down the problem into its basic layers or components.

Thought Leaders: Identify what leaders and experts are saying about the issue.

Context/Culture: Identify how culture impacts people's views of the problem.

Questions: Question all assumptions, popular beliefs and the obvious.

Observations: Pay close attention to leaders, ideas, headlines, market trends and government regulations related to the problem.

Reading: Read intensively on the problem.

The framework above is not exhaustive and presents concrete steps you can take to build your own FPT game plan. However, you should use your best judgment to apply these strategies because your thinking and actions may vary depending on your workplace or business context, situation and culture.

Allow us to elaborate on some key strategies.

The first step toward using this skill successfully is realizing when you're approaching a problem through the lens of past experiences and an over-reliance on pre-existing beliefs.

Practice is the key to developing the ability to think in first principles. Constructing an argument based on first principles requires experience and self-awareness, which you can only gain through practice. As with any skill, the more you use your capability to think in first principles, the better you will become at it.

FPT enables us to question our beliefs and assess them accurately by forcing us to think about how they work under different conditions. We may find that what we believe to be true most of the time is false or incomplete in particular situations.

Analyzing your assumptions also facilitates innovation because it allows you to develop new approaches rather than simply using existing methods.

The best way to hone this skill is through deliberate practice. You systematically study and improve your current knowledge of FPT by answering questions about the fundamentals rather than the details. This will help you become better at noticing when your perspective on a problem is limited because it's based too much on experience or belief.

One good way to develop FPT skills is by using thought experiments that involve imagining yourself in a totally different situation and questioning what you take for granted about reality.

For instance, if you're working as an assistant for someone who manages other employees, imagine how things would be different if you were managing everything yourself. Without prior experience, you question everything you thought was true about being a manager and rethink your perspective using first principles.

First Principles Thinking Vs. Incremental Thinking

FPT is the opposite of incremental thinking. Incremental thinkers look at what has been done before, use those past

SYSTEMS: USING FIRST PRINCIPLES THINKING

successes as guidelines for developing new ideas and solutions, and take small steps forward. They like rules that guide behavior, and they like standard operating procedures (SOPs) for similar processes, because:

- They don't have to reinvent the wheel every time.
- Standards make it easy.
- Standards provide safety.
- Standards prevent mistakes.
- It keeps them from falling back into their old ways.

First Principles Thinking is quite the opposite. To develop FPT skills and ability, think about how children learn. Young children learn by connecting their actions with the immediate consequences of those actions. Children repeat behaviors that bring positive outcomes or things they like or find interesting. They avoid behaviors that bring negative outcomes or things they don't like or find uninteresting. They are basically learning machines. They have no fear of failure—just curiosity and the initiative to try new things.

Rather than starting with the current paradigm and trying to tweak things within that box or narrow perspective, FPT encourages you to think about an issue completely differently. The goal is to tap into your imagination and really think outside the box—or even eliminate the box! By using this type of thinking, you can suggest new ideas that may never have been considered because they don't fit into the usual way of thinking.

Many people are not even aware that there are different ways to think about something. Sometimes, basing your ideas, opinions and solutions on previous information—or what you've been told or taught in the past—can be a hindrance if it's not relevant to the current situation. While some information might still be helpful, changing how you think about something could lead you in a completely new direction.

When an issue seems difficult to grasp or mull over, further analysis will complicate things more unless you improve your understanding. FPT encourages breaking down an idea into its fundamental components so that new possibilities can emerge with less effort. The goal is to get back to basics—the fundamentals–to grasp what's essential and build from there.

Strategies for Developing First Principles Thinking Skills and Abilities

FPT is a rational technique that uses reason to construct or discover the essence of a topic by thinking about its most fundamental aspects. It's an important capability in business because it can:

- Help create new ideas and solutions.
- Identify risks.
- Solve stubborn problems.
- Innovate.
- Handle change successfully.
- Address key decisions effectively.

Knowing how to think like this can also help you land jobs or promotions when people are looking for innovative thinkers with fresh ideas that are less constrained by conventional wisdom—someone able to look beyond what everyone else is doing and focus on what really matters.

Some strategies for developing First Principles Thinking include:

> **Learning to think about the fundamentals.**
> Most people, including most leaders and managers, don't focus enough on these and spend too much time doing things that aren't important. Many problems we face in business stem from this simple fact—we need to rethink what is fundamental and re-organize around these.

> **Identifying correlations between seemingly unrelated phenomena.**
> Figure out where ideas can be combined or how things work together. Different examples of applying First Principles Thinking include J. P. Morgan's development of derivatives, Ford's productivity improvements after ending its divisional structure and creating new markets similar to Google with Gmail and Android.

> **Thinking in terms of first principles.**
> First Principles are foundational truths not derived from other ideas or concepts. Once you grasp the concept of a first principle, it is easier to grasp lesser derivative principles. Think of this as learning to use grammar before learning words, sentences and paragraphs.

The Benefits of First Principles Thinking

FPT is a mental shift that helps to unlock your future. If you are an individual or company that wants to expand, gain a competitive advantage, or gain momentum, FPT may be the answer.

The benefits of First principles Thinking include:

- Building skills like critical thinking, creativity and rationality into your team, allowing them to envision new growth opportunities.
- Capitalizing on innovations with greater ease by generating creative solutions that are potentially higher in value than the sum of their parts (like an innovation leapfrog effect).
- Advantageous strategic positioning relative to competitors, which is achieved by differentiating your offering, business model and strategy from the pack.
- Flexible thinking as companies can explore new business models, develop more effective mission statements, and make more informed decisions about managing finances, people and operations.
- Gaining a competitive edge over rivals by considering singular points of view that transcend market conventions.

By internalizing FPT logically within yourself, you develop more clarity about how the world works. You better understand cause and effect, and therefore, you better understand consequences for your actions and decision-making process. This clarity brings greater confidence in who you are and what you do.

In turn, that confidence allows you to be bolder in your actions and decision-making process. Instead of being a person who lives life passively, you become a person who proactively acts and shapes their future and destiny.

Developing FPT skills is about developing clarity within yourself. Be clear on what you want in your life, the future you want to create for yourself, and understand how the world works so you can better understand cause and effect. Once you develop this clarity, it will bring greater confidence in who you are, allowing you to be bolder with your actions and decision-making processes!

CHAPTER VII
How to Use First Principles Thinking in Your Personal Life to Stand Out

"Think simple' as my old master used to say - meaning reduce the whole of its parts into the simplest terms, getting back to first principles."-

— FRANK LLOYD WRIGHT

At work, school and in business, we constantly need to advance. We must continue to set higher goals for ourselves and use these guideposts to measure our progress and guide us toward future accomplishments. It's a universal part of life.

Using FPT can help you stand out in your personal life. It allows you to come up with new ideas by inverting conventional wisdom and thinking about a problem in a completely differently. Many success stories have resounded throughout history because people decided to think outside the box using First Principles Thinking.

In this chapter, you'll discover how you can use First Principles Thinking in your personal life with a few practical examples.

How to Use First Principles Thinking in Your Personal Life

You can use First Principles Thinking to develop new ideas in your personal life. Sometimes, creativity is about simplifying something complicated so that other people can understand it more easily.

Applying FPT can simplify complex problems so everyone can better understand them or unfurl existing ideas.

Reverse Engineering Solutions to Problems

FPT is the opposite of working backward. When problem-solving, people tend to work with what they know instead of trying to find out what is unknown. Sometimes, this works fine because it helps narrow down options. However, new ideas sometimes come from exploring possibilities instead of limitations.

When faced with a difficult question or challenge, try to use First Principles Thinking by finding new questions that are interesting or have more angles for exploration. Look at things from different perspectives until you can see connections that other people cannot easily spot.

Examining your assumptions on certain topics is also helpful in FPT as you discover more about how things work within broader contexts.

To reverse engineer a solution to your problem, take a step back and look at the problem itself. Think of ways other people have solved similar problems before or find reference points for new perspectives. FPT allows you to see creative solutions by looking beyond existing constraints, thereby helping you make better decisions in life.

Questioning the Process

You can think more innovatively when you take a step back and question the process rather than focus on your preconceived notions.

By removing yourself from whatever current situation or problem you face, you'll gain a new perspective on approaching it. Before trying to problem-solve, ask yourself, "What am I assuming?" This makes it easier to look at an issue from multiple perspectives.

The goal is not just originality but also simplicity. When people think creatively, they often try to develop more complex solutions. However, FPT allows people to find the most straightforward solution because it isn't clouded by convention or popular assumptions.

This simple approach to problems allows people from many disciplines to create new and innovative ideas. In business, this type of thinking can be a powerful tool for advancing your career. FPT allows you to make a unique impact in a field by taking a fresh perspective on the norms of that space. Some examples of people who've used FPT include:

> **Henry Ford, the founder of Ford Motor Company**
> Ford developed an assembly line that revolutionized car manufacturing and increased productivity tremendously. He didn't just adopt the status quo way of building cars but looked at things through FPT and developed a process that transformed the entire manufacturing sector.

> **Steve Jobs**
> Steve popularized user-friendly computers with his work on Apple computers. He approached computers from the standpoint of a person outside of the computing industry. He saw things from a different lens, which furthered the development of user-friendly technology that was around at the time.

> **Elon Musk**
> Musk realized that electric car technologies would improve in leaps and bounds over time. Therefore, he started his own company, Tesla Inc., which produces high-performance electric cars. He took concepts from multiple industries where electric cars were being used effectively and brought them together to create a world-changing innovation.

All these people did something to set themselves apart from others in their field. The next question is "How does one acquire this thinking when trying to advance professionally or when looking to make exciting business ideas?"

FPT is the process of getting back to the basics so that one can use first principles. It can be done with key principles applied to any industry. Often, when people are focused on making money or advancing their career, they lose touch with the process that got them there and continue with patterns of thought-based strategy that they used previously.

How Can I Stand Out in My Personal Life with First Principles Thinking?

When people are advancing their careers or trying to make money, they tend to rely on "tried and true" methods for success instead of identifying the first principles behind what got them there. This means that instead of starting with an idea or making something unique, they begin by trying to imitate others who have succeeded previously. After all, it's often easier to follow someone else's path than to blaze your own.

While imitation of others is essential, it should not be blind, imitating strategies that ignore how those strategies came about and for what they were used. FPT allows people to understand what needs to be accomplished, rather than copying other people's ideas and working from there.

This form of thinking is complicated for most people to master, so it may be necessary to work on certain aspects of your life that you already feel have a strong foundation. The best way to do this would be to find things that are currently

SYSTEMS: USING FIRST PRINCIPLES THINKING

working well in your personal or professional life and try to use FPT with them.

For example, you may enjoy the work that you do, but that doesn't mean you can't think about ways that you could approach problems differently than others!

By using FPT in your personal life, you may experience various positive changes. For example, if you currently feel like your life is filled with problems that you're unable to solve, then FPT may be able to give you the tools that you need. Ask yourself, "What's actually holding me back?" This way of thinking allows you to break down your problem into smaller sections and produce results that will help move things forward and motivate you!

Of course, FPT can also cause negative changes in your personal life. It is very easy to get carried away with FPT—especially on something that is causing a lot of pain or discomfort. If this happens, it may be beneficial to take a step back and look at the bigger picture. In this case, asking yourself, "What's actually holding me back?" may not be what you want to hear!

In terms of career advancement, using FPT could help move you in the right direction. Reinvention is an excellent way to take your current position and re-imagine it into something that works better for you.

For example, your current job involves creating media campaigns for clients. If this isn't going too well, applying FPT would allow you to brainstorm other ways your role might work better for you. Perhaps you can work with smaller businesses or even older demographics who may not be as quick to adopt new marketing methods.

You can also apply FPT to your personal life. Say you're interested in getting involved with a certain social group but have been rejected because you didn't have the right haircut or shoes. FPT would allow you to take a step back and look at why people might not be accepting of you. Are they judging solely by appearance? If so, then this isn't much of a personal issue. It's more about their own judgmental attitude, which has nothing to do with who you are.

Here's how you can use FPT in your life.

Learn as much as possible about a topic before trying to solve a problem within that domain. Don't assume you know what you're talking about, even if everyone else does—because they might all be wrong!

Instead, take a step back and try to approach the problem without any preconceptions. This approach will involve gathering information from multiple sources and synthesizing them into a single viewpoint—which is often something new. In other words, you're not looking at the same thing everyone else is; you're challenging assumptions and breaking things down to their basic components.

When thinking about problems in your career, don't assume there's only one way to solve them. Most people will try to push their opinions on you, but this is rarely helpful if your gut instinct tells you something different.

Go back to the first principles and start from scratch. Ask yourself exactly what's holding you back and why. How can you recursively break that problem into smaller pieces? What other options do you have? You should always challenge everything: your opinions, other people's assumptions and even what seems like common sense!

No matter who you are, how well-off you are or what position you hold, you can always learn something from FPT that will allow personal development and career advancement.

Using FPT is an effective way of helping yourself find solutions within your day-to-day activities. By taking a step back and examining the root cause of an issue—first principles—you can gain a higher-level point of view that allows you to see the bigger picture.

CHAPTER VIII

How to Stand Out Using First Principles Thinking in Your Professional and Business Life

"The world is filled with unimaginative, copycat solutions. These predictably lead to linear outcomes. Leveraging first principles thinking is intense and time consuming—but it is also a pathway to devising creative solutions that drive non-linear, asymmetric outcomes."-

— SAHIL BLOOM

FPT was first conceived by the Greek philosopher, Aristotle, as an expansion of Plato's Theory of Forms. This theory is based on the foundational concepts from which all things originate and on which all things are built. It is based on those aspects that make something true and central to its existence (the nature of a thing) and those actions that describe its fundamental purpose (what something does). It's a way of looking at and understanding reality.

You can use First Principles Thinking in your professional and business life to stand out in your career by assessing your current situation, identifying what isn't working and why, and devising how to address the problem using new approaches based on what's actually happening.

FPT can be used to think through any challenge you face professionally or in business. In this chapter, we provide steps to use FPT in your business life.

How to Stand Out in Your Professional and Business Life with First Principles Thinking

Having an action plan is essential in life and business, especially if you want to develop the skill of thinking about first principles. If you do not know the end goal, it becomes challenging to determine where to focus your attention or what questions to ask yourself. You cannot solve problems that you do not anticipate. Without an end goal in mind, it can be hard to determine which questions need answering and how they will get you what you desire.

Applying these principles requires the following:

- An effective evaluation of the problem at hand
- Clarifying the problem by asking questions
- Breaking down each element into its simplest parts
- Creating a solution to the problem and questioning the process

This level of thinking is especially valuable if you are working on a problem that has not been solved before or in which initial assumptions about the problem are incorrect.

FPT allows you to re-examine everything with fresh eyes so you can determine where your assumptions were wrong, whether there was an error in your reasoning, which part of the process contains opportunities for improvement, and how far back you need to go to understand why things occurred the way they did.

By questioning basic assumptions instead of relying on them, FPT also helps foster creativity. You will be able to open possibilities that might not have otherwise occurred to you because you are actively seeking out where you might have misinterpreted information.

Thinking about first principles will allow you to use your experience and expertise more effectively and consider what is truly most important instead of continuing along a path because of the time, energy and effort it would supposedly take to deviate from it.

Let's look at some concrete steps to problem-solving with FPT in a business and professional setting.

1. Start by defining your problem.

First Principles Thinking starts with a strategy for approaching a problem by reconceptualizing its foundational elements or characteristics from scratch. This means looking at things differently by considering their core purpose to find an original solution.

When applying FPT, the first step is to understand the situation. This involves breaking down complicated problems into their individual parts to analyze them better and determine what knowledge already exists about them.

You can then identify any given scenario by looking for patterns in data related to the problem.

Be sure to break down the issue into its most basic components, so you have something simple to work with, and you can separate assumptions from facts. Begin by writing everything down on paper or typing it into a document so there are no constraints on what ideas might come next during later stages of the process.

You might need to ask yourself questions like:

- Why do we have these particular parts?
- Do they really work together?
- What happens if I remove one of the parts?

To apply FPT to your business problems, start by looking at issues within your business where you or your team may be repeating mistakes or making things more difficult than they should be. Once identified, choose the most important and immediate one to address first.

2. Clarify the problem.

Once you have identified the root cause of your business problem, the next step is to generate as many solutions as possible to resolve it, without being inhibited by any critical factors such as time and budgetary constraints. You must think outside of the box because creativity requires stepping away from what is already known to identify new ways to do things that will lead you out of trouble.

Consider all the possibilities, even seemingly outrageous ones, because they just might work if addressed properly. Do this exercise in the mindset of an inventor because living in that space will allow you to explore all possibilities and increase your potential for generating out-of-the-box solutions.

FPT is different from other forms of reasoning because it requires you to develop core principles that you can apply across different areas. By setting aside what you currently know about a problem, you can explore new or alternative approaches until you identify something original rather than simply refining existing knowledge. By doing this, you come up with genuinely novel solutions and ideas, which may ultimately lead to increased productivity.

Using the Five Whys Method of First Principles Thinking to Break Down the Problem

When using FPT, use the "5 Whys" method to help you drill down to the core principles.

The "5 Whys" is a simple but powerful tool for finding the root cause of issues in business development. When faced with an issue, finding the source can be difficult or time-consuming without first asking the relevant questions.

Using the "5 Whys" method involves repeating the question "Why?" five times, moving one level deeper into an explanation each time. For example:

1. **Why did our sales drop?** Sales dropped because we didn't meet our target numbers last quarter.

2. **Why didn't we hit our target numbers?** We sold 23% less than expected because sales were off by 8%.
3. **Why were sales off by 8%?** Sales were off because we came under budget across all categories.
4. **Why did we come under budget?** We spent less money because there was a surplus of items this year due to a mild winter season.
5. **Why did we have a mild winter season?** Because last year's winter was harsh and forced retailers to stock up on supplies, which led to extra inventory this year.

This is a simplistic example, but its simplicity allows the focus to stay on finding the root cause or "whys" rather than getting lost down the rabbit hole. This is especially useful when many people are involved in finding answers within an organization; no one person can cover all angles alone, and different people may focus on different areas, leading to information gaps or even conflicts.

Once the root cause is identified, think about how you would ideally like things to be with the issue. This ideal state may not yet exist, and it may not even be possible, but you should aim high since trying to improve something will bring better results than just trying to do a quick fix.

Solving the Problem and Questioning the Process

Once you have identified and broken down the problem, it should be easier to solve. Most problems consist of several sub-problems and deciding on the best way to attack those sub-problems will bring about the best solution.

It is possible that multiple solutions have equal value, and it might take time for you to determine which is the best fit, given your resources and constraints. Having several possibilities allows you to test them out against each other to maximize gains while minimizing the effort expended on each option. This can save time and resources and allow for the opportunity to come up with even better alternatives.

FPT relies on questioning the process, not using prior assumptions. The process is repeated until you begin to see patterns that help guide your next round of questioning. If you pay attention, these guiding principles will reveal themselves over time and will not require outside information or expertise to determine.

Some tips when using FPT in a business setting include:

- **Avoiding pre-judgments and assumptions**
  Be skeptical about facts that have not been empirically tested.
- **Embracing being wrong or admitting ignorance**
  It is part of being human to be fallible, and therefore, it is only logical to embrace your fallibility as a strength rather than a weakness. To learn, you must challenge ideas and question facts – this lets you grow intellectually and personally.
- **Understanding how things work on a fundamental level**
  Without any outside influence, understanding the fundamental level allows you to separate emotion

from the situation and make decisions logically instead of emotionally.

- **Not accepting claims or statements as fact**
  Don't accept claims as fact until they have been empirically tested.

- **Considering your own fallibility and the possibility of being wrong**
  We do not consider ourselves infallible. We are humans with human frailties and faults—this should be equally applied when considering other people's ideas and mistakes. In doing so, your ability to assess another person's point of view will increase significantly, helping build rapport and understanding between two parties involved in an argument.

FPT can be a useful tool for managing your career and business life. It is a way of solving problems by taking things back to their most fundamental truths. You go beyond the conventional wisdom and analysis of an issue to get back to the basics.

Research, Tools and Other Resources on First Principles Thinking

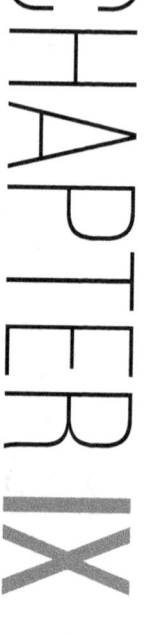

"When you simply ignore the box and build your reasoning from scratch, whether you're brilliant or not, you end up with a unique conclusion—one that may or may not fall within the box."

— *TIM URBAN*

First Principles Thinking is a simple yet powerful philosophy that can help you succeed in your career and business. It's the process of thinking about every idea, problem or situation by first questioning your underlying assumptions and starting with a blank slate to find a better answer.

Learning how to use FPT to meet your career objectives is no easy task; as we've noted, it takes practice. Luckily, you can find many books and websites on the topic that will help you learn how to use this technique. Here are some of the top books for learning more about FPT:

Aristotle's First Principles by Terence Irwin

Aristotle's First Principles provides a fresh interpretation of Aristotle's most fundamental metaphysical treatise: his work on first principles. Irwin explains the components of Aristotle's theory of being, examines his arguments in detail, and explores the impact of his work on later philosophers.

This is an excellent book on Aristotle's philosophical approach and the benefits of his conclusions. Irwin demonstrates how Aristotle opposed dialectic, asserting that it can't support a metaphysical realist's claims. Instead, he emphasizes the connections between ideas that are frequently treated as distinct.

Aristotle's philosophy is relevant today in several topics, especially the way it influences other philosophers such as Gottfried Leibniz, who was not only a philosopher but also one of the best mathematicians in history. There are significant comparisons between his work on this subject and Aristotle's.

Aristotle's relation with Plato is also discussed in depth since they were students together. However, they ended their relationship when Aristotle disagreed with Plato on various philosophical principles regarding dialectic methods. The purpose of each method has been debated for many centuries by philosophers worldwide because it seems to have different purposes according to who is using them. This book shows how Aristotle used dialectics successfully when he wanted to prove things about animals or other natural phenomena.

First Principles: What America's Founders Learned from the Greeks and Romans and How That Shaped Our Country by Thomas E. Ricks

First Principles: What America's Founders Learned from the Greeks and Romans and How That Shaped Our Country is a book on the political philosophy that inspired America's founders and shaped our country today. Ricks describes the context of Ancient Greece and Rome, discussing why they were considered important by the Founding Fathers and what principles from the ancient world influenced modern America.

Ricks uses the example of the first self-sufficient American colony, how they modeled themselves on Plato's Republic, and the lessons they learned from their mistakes. He also relates how Thomas Jefferson adapted Ancient Greek architecture to modern building plans.

Ricks also discusses how today's political situation is divided so there is a need to find shared first principles across party lines for a unified society. He outlines these shared principles and recommends more study on classical texts to improve shared understanding.

Thinking, Fast and Slow by Daniel Kahneman

Thinking, Fast and Slow is a book on how we think and make decisions. The author explains the difference between our

SYSTEMS: USING FIRST PRINCIPLES THINKING

"system one" or fast thinking and "system two" or slow thinking, and the pitfalls of each type of system. Kahneman uses well-known examples to demonstrate how predictable our "system one" thinking is and how well we can predict the outcome of a situation based on primitive factors. Additionally, Kahneman uses less well-known examples to show how poorly we predict the outcome of a situation based on "system two" thinking.

The most important takeaways from this book are that you can accurately predict many situations by using "system one" thinking, that you should never assume your "system two" thinking is correct, and that all biases exist for a reason.

First Principles Thinking Workbook: Framework for Solving Real-Life Problems Using First Principles Thinking Technique by Sperikon Innovative Books

This workbook outlines the principles and framework used for fast thinking to help people solve problems in their work and daily lives. This book is an excellent resource for those looking to enhance their problem-solving skills but do not have the time or knowledge to enroll in a complete executive education program.

First Principles Thinking is a framework that will help you solve problems, whether they are straightforward or complex. With FPT, there are no constraints in using pre-defined theories or mental models. When solving a problem, the only thing that matters is thinking about the thought process instead of focusing on the solution itself. This book provides an outline for understanding the most important components in FPT practice.

Strategic Intuition: The Creative Spark in Human Achievement by William Duggan

William Duggan's seminal book on creative thinking, *Strategic Intuition*, thoroughly introduces First Principles. According to Duggan, the core of this mindset is to change your thinking of the state of things as being composed of a system of relationships between parts or elements, which are defined by their functions in relation to each other. Rather, it is a collection of parts or elements standing in some definite relationship to a purpose.

Duggan says this way of thinking takes you "outside" the normal way of seeing things. It frees you from your assumptions about how things should be done and allows you to focus on finding new solutions.

Zero to One by Peter Thiel

Peter Thiel's book, *Zero to One*, is one of the most popular business books of the last few years, and it is an excellent illustration of how FPT can be applied. Thiel is a thought leader in the technology industry, both as an investor and a thought leader. His book is based on his observations about why software companies succeed and fail in today's economy. He starts with the fundamental truth that you can only compete on one axis—price, quality or features.

The most important thing to understand about FPT is that you cannot force it; reasoning from first principles never arrives at logical conclusions or viable strategies by accident.

SYSTEMS: USING FIRST PRINCIPLES THINKING

Instead, your intuition must guide you towards the fundamental truths of any given problem. Before you can apply reason to discover solutions using a first-principles approach, ask yourself, "What are they limiting me to?"

Thiel's book helps guide young entrepreneurs along paths they may not have considered before using the FPT process. The method encourages people to think about what underlying fundamentals exist now and then build something new by focusing on these fundamentals rather than conventional wisdom.

Thiel focuses on creating value that did not exist before and competing on a new axis instead of tweaking something that already exists. This approach requires a unique insight into business opportunities, and Thiel offers examples of how young entrepreneurs have achieved them in various ways.

Tools for First Principles Thinking Application

The first principles method is the same process that Elon Musk uses at SpaceX, which aims to radically reduce space transportation costs so that humans can become multi-planetary species within our lifetimes. It's also the same process Steve Jobs used to develop ideas for Apple. The following are some tools that you can use to facilitate your FPT process.

Untools' First Principles Thinking Tool

Untools is a collection of thinking tools and frameworks to help you solve problems, make decisions and understand systems. Untools has a feature for FPT and is one of the only apps on the market that helps you apply FPT to your day-to-day life.

Untools helps you understand complex problems and arrive at solutions. The app can be used as a thinking companion to help you tackle tough problems by breaking them apart into their components, solving each part, and then reassembling information to find a solution.

Mentorist

The Mentorist app is a tool used to find mentors from across the country. It helps entrepreneurs and those who want to become more experienced in their field find people who can guide them as they develop as professionals. The app allows users to search by location, industry, company size or skill set and connect with that person on social media platforms such as LinkedIn or Facebook. It's intended to facilitate real-world relationships. After establishing that initial connection, you will need to meet face-to-face and establish a personal rapport before receiving actual mentoring support.

Mentorist has a program influenced by Elon Musk. It provides a platform for developing a small business by allowing people to work through the process as if they were doing an internship. The app provides advice on FPT. Essentially, the program helps others think like Musk and considering that he is successful thus far, it's hard to argue with this logic.

The Mentorist app can be used in conjunction with other apps such as Skillshare and Upwork to gain real-world experience and use that experience in interviews when seeking employment or getting more clients for your small business.

Videos and Podcasts Covering First Principles Thinking

Exponential Wisdom, a podcast featuring many different leaders in the technology industry, is another place to go if you're looking for more information on FPT. Their episodes include one with best-selling author Peter Diamandis, in which he discusses the concept of solving problems by rethinking them at a high level and digging deep into all assumptions instead of fixing things incrementally.

Another podcast specializing in long-form discussion includes Masters of Scale, which features an episode with Reed Hastings, CEO of Netflix, who talks about the value of distilling your objectives to their most basic forms to help you accomplish them more efficiently.

Courses on First Principles Thinking

Factory for Innovative Policy Solutions offers a course covering FPT. This course dives into how you can overcome the status quo bias prevalent in organizations today.

This course will give you a new perspective on how to push through resistance and move your business forward as it offers complete coverage of this method of thinking, from its origin to its modern-day applications.

YouTube Video Interviews with Elon Musk and Other Thought Leaders

YouTube is one of the best resources for learning about FPT. There is a wide variety of interviews that feature business leaders, including Elon Musk. These are great resources to help you become more familiar with First Principles Thinking and its applications in the modern world.

When facing a problem with no available solutions, try thinking of it as a problem of first principles. It's worked for Elon Musk, so there's no reason it won't work for you too! YouTube differs from other resources because it provides interviews directly from those that practice FPT like Musk and others. The YouTube interview "The First Principles Method Explained by Elon Musk" by Kevin Rose is an excellent example of the kind of fundamental questions Musk asks himself when designing new inventions or businesses.

A more philosophical resource for First Principles Thinking comes from the YouTube interview, "Elon Musk first principles reasoning TED." In this interview, Musk explains that although something might not have been done before, it doesn't mean that you can't do it now. He uses the example of putting a man on Mars, which hasn't been successfully done by NASA yet. Musk approaches this by thinking about the problem differently from what had already been tried unsuccessfully in the past.

SYSTEMS: USING FIRST PRINCIPLES THINKING

Elon Musk utilizes FPT to push through the various barriers that stand between people and their goals. According to Musk, this process involves four steps:

1. Recognizing which parts of your beliefs are factually incorrect
2. De-scoping or removing any external factors that may be clouding your judgment
3. Brainstorming new ways to achieve your desired outcome using only the information you have
4. Testing out these new theories to determine if they work

Videos from other thought leaders, including Peter Thiel, Marc Andreessen and Sam Altman, are also available on YouTube. These videos show the process of FPT in action and provide a glimpse into what kinds of thoughts go through the heads of successful innovators and business leaders as they employ this critical mode of thinking.

For example, a great business resource for First Principles Thinking comes from Peter Thiel, who details his way of thinking in his YouTube interview, "Peter Thiel: Going from Zero to One." He explains the necessity of ignoring all previous knowledge and creating original solutions based on first principles only. He also discusses the importance of people who think this way in an organization, often called "Founders," who can challenge assumptions.

The resources available on FPT are valuable tools for anyone looking to improve their thought process, combat cognitive biases, overcome the fear of failure, and push the boundaries of normal productivity.

All the resources we mentioned will give you an additional understanding of using First Principles Thinking in your personal, business and professional life.

CONCLUSION

> *"First principles are foundational truths."*
> **- Sahil Bloom**

First Principles Thinking is not a magic solution; it's a new way of thinking that can take time for you to get accustomed. However, it's worth the effort because it's an approach to approaching problems empirically and logically so you can move your career or business to new heights. As you know, the marketplace is competitive and crowded with traditional thinking and boring services. Therefore, following best practices and standard operating procedures (SOPs) to solve problems won't help you stand out. Doing so is a sure way to get swallowed by the harsh competition.

Therefore, if you want to be different and enjoy different results, you need to investigate problems in depth by questioning obvious and popular beliefs.

The concrete examples of the positive impact of FPT show how you can apply it to become a thought leader and a trailblazer in your line of work or business.

However, we hope you won't talk about and use FPT just for the sake of sounding cool and intellectual. Doing so would be a waste of your time since it will lead you nowhere. Rather, we recommend you use FPT as a tool to take concrete actions to make a difference in your world— and the world around you!

We hope that the framework and resources we've provided on FPT will help you get started on your journey of becoming an innovative problem solver. Take advantage of them to further your understanding of the topic. Read the resources, check out the strategies and use the tools we've provided to create your framework to develop and use FPT in different areas of your life.

We've shown you how you to use FPT to further your professional dreams. We did our part, and now it's your turn to act and make a difference in your life.

Please do us one small favor: Please gift this book to a friend or anyone you know who wants to stand out from the crowd.

REFERENCES

Duggan, W. R. (2013). *Strategic intuition: The creative spark in human achievement.* Columbia Business School Publishing.

Irwin, T. (1990). *Aristotle's first principles.* Oxford University Press.

Kahneman, D. (2013). *Thinking, fast and slow.* Farrar, Straus and Giroux.

Kraut, R. (1997). *Plato's Republic.* Rowman & Littlefield.

Ricks, T. E. (2020). *First principles: What America's founders learned from the Greeks and Romans and how that shaped our country.* Harper.

Sperikon Innovative Books. (2021). *First principles thinking workbook: Framework for solving real-life problems using first principles thinking technique.*

Thiel, P., & Masters, B. (2014). *Zero to one: Notes on startups, or how to build the future.* Crown Business.

INDEX

A

Amazon 14, 15, 21, 22, 31
Apple 38, 53, 71
Aristotle 7, 19, 58, 67, 79
assumptions.. 3, 6, 7, 12, 13, 14, 18, 21, 23, 24, 26, 29, 30, 31, 32, 35, 37, 38, 39, 40, 43, 44, 52, 56, 57, 59, 60, 61, 64, 66, 70, 73, 75

B

best practices... 2, 14, 33, 41, 77

C

critical thinking 3, 21, 22, 24, 48

D

Daniel Kahneman 68
deductive reasoning 6, 7

E

Elon Musk.. 6, 7, 12, 13, 14, 15, 16, 19, 20, 28, 30, 39, 53, 71, 72, 74, 75
employees . 4, 13, 14, 21, 27, 34, 35, 36, 38, 40, 44

F

first philosophy 7
first principles reasoning 20, 74
first-order reasoning 29
Five Whys Method 62
Ford Motor Company 53
Founders Fund 22
framework.. 4, 8, 20, 42, 43, 44, 69, 78, 79
fundamental principles 8, 13

G

Google 17, 38, 47
Gottfried Leibniz 67

H

Henry Ford 53

I

inductive reasoning 6, 7
Isadore Sharp 32

J

J. P. Morgan 47
Jeff Bezos 14, 19, 21, 22, 31

L

Larry Page 38

M

Marc Andreessen 75

N

Netflix 73
Neuralink 20

P

Palantir Technologies 22
Paypal 31
Peter Diamandis 73
Peter Thiel 12, 19, 22, 23, 70, 75
Plato 58, 67, 68, 79
problem-solving ... 8, 10, 21, 22, 24, 41, 51, 60, 69
product architect approach 8
professionals .. 1, 2, 3, 4, 14, 34, 35, 36, 37, 40, 42, 72, 82

R

Reed Hastings 73
Reverse Engineering 51
Richard Feynman 19, 23

S

Sergey Brin 38
SpaceX 12, 16, 20, 31, 40, 71
Steve Jobs 53, 71

T

Terence Irwin 67
Tesla 7, 12, 13, 14, 15, 20, 21, 30, 31, 39, 53
Theory of Forms 58
Thomas E. Ricks 68
Thomas Jefferson 68

W

William Duggan 70

ABOUT CBL
COACHING FOR BETTER LEARNING

CBL helps build Continuous Improvement (CI) systems that lead to stress-free improvement, growth and sustainable success.

We offer reliable client-centered systems building coaching services to help you face your challenges with more confidence and less anxiety. Visit us at

coachingforbetterlearning.com

Check our blog out:

https://coachingforbetterlearning.com/blog.

Also by CBL

- ➢ Creating Winning Career Systems
- ➢ System: Using Contrarian Thinking to Power Your Career or Business Engine

www.ingramcontent.com/pod-product-compliance
Lightning Source LLC
Chambersburg PA
CBHW070301220526
45465CB00004B/1691